WITHDRAWN

Mosaics

Nathaniel Harris

PowerKiDS
press.

New York

Published in 2009 by The Rosen Publishing Group Inc.
29 East 21st Street, New York, NY 10010

First Edition

Senior Editor: Claire Shanahan
Designer: Rachel Hamdi/Holly Fulbrook
Project Maker: Anna-Marie d'Cruz
Models: Zachary O' Brien Miller, Katie Powell
Photographer: Andy Crawford
Thanks to Suvianna Leivo, p25.

Library of Congress Cataloging-in-Publication Data

Harris, Nathaniel, 1937-
  Mosaics / Nathaniel Harris. — 1st ed.
     p. cm. — (Stories in art)
  Includes index.
  ISBN 978-1-4042-4438-2 (library binding)
  1. Mosaics—Juvenile literature. 2. Mosaics—Technique—Juvenile literature. I. Title. II. Series.

  NA3750.H36 2009
  738.5—dc22

2007052714

Title page, p12/13: North by Northwest, one of 17 mosaics that make up the "Hitchcock Gallery" at
Leytonstone Tube Station. Designed and created by Greenwich Mural Workshop. Can be seen at
www.greenwichmuralworkshop.com; p6: The dome of the Masjid-i-Sheikh Lutfallah, built 1602–19 by Shah
Abbas I (faience mosaic) by Islamic School, (seventeenth century), Isfahan, Iran/The Bridgeman Art Library;
p7: Two-headed serpent pectoral, 1400–1520 AD (wood decorated with turquoise & shell mosaic) by Aztec,
British Museum, London, U.K./The Bridgeman Art Library; p8: © John Heseltine/Corbis; p9: Lynne Chinn &
Shug Jones; p10/11, front page: The Alexander Mosaic, depicting the Battle of Issus between Alexander
the Great (356–323 BC) and Darius III (d.330 BC) in 333 BC, Roman floor mosaic removed from the Casa del
Fauno (House of the Faun) at Pompeii (mosaic) (see 71311) by Roman (first century BC), Museo
Archeologico Nazionale, Naples, Italy/Alinari/The Bridgeman Art Library; p14/15: The Judgement of Paris,
from the House of the Atrium, Antioch, ca. 115 AD (mosaic) by Roman, (second century AD), Louvre, Paris,
France/The Bridgeman Art Library; p16/17: Noah taking the Animals into the Ark, mosaic in the Vestibule
of San Marco, Venice by San Marco, Venice, Italy/ Francesco Turio Bohm/The Bridgeman Art Library;
p18/19: Defiance by Boris Anrep. Photo © The National Gallery, London; p210/21: Ulysses and the Sirens
(mosaic) by Roman, (third century AD), Musee du Bardo, Tunis, Tunisia/ Giraudon/The Bridgeman Art
Library.

Manufactured in China

Contents

What are mosaics?

A mosaic is a special kind of artwork. It is made up of small colored pieces, arranged side by side to create a picture or pattern. The pieces are most often colored stones or glass. When they are stuck down or set in cement, the picture becomes a very solid object. Some examples in this book have survived all kinds of upheavals—even volcanic eruptions—for 2,000 years.

The toughness of mosaics gives them important advantages. They can be put up outdoors, in exposed public places. They also make remarkably hard-wearing floor surfaces. Literally millions of visitors to the National Gallery in London have walked on the 50-year-old *Defiance* mosaic on page 18! Inside buildings, mosaics make striking wall and ceiling decorations.

Past and present

Mosaics have a long history. Five thousand years ago, people in the Middle East were creating patterns on walls by pressing pieces of clay into them. Later, artists in Islamic societies put up dazzling mosaic domes and filled other surfaces with **abstract** or flower patterns. Across the Atlantic, the Aztecs of Mexico and other peoples covered objects, such as figures and masks, with mosaics of turquoise and other semiprecious stones.

▲ *The dome of the Sheikh Lotfallah Mosque in Isfahan, Iran. Dating from the early sixteenth century, it is covered with superb mosaics.*

The ancient Greeks founded a different tradition. They made mosaics that were pictures of people and animals, often shown in scenes that were part of a story. Then the Romans took up mosaic-making and spread it all over their vast empire. Many Greek and Roman mosaics have scenes from the stories they most enjoyed, such as **myths** and legends about gods and heroes and long-ago wars. For centuries after the Roman Empire was converted to Christianity, mosaics were used lavishly in churches to tell biblical stories.

In recent times, mosaics have often been chosen for large-scale decorations on public buildings. Look at the floors and walls of town halls, museums, and libraries—you will be surprised by how often you see a mosaic you hadn't noticed before. Nowadays, mosaic artists work in all kinds of styles, often to decorate houses or gardens. The ancient art of mosaic is as popular as ever.

▲ *This two-headed serpent, covered with turquoise and shell mosaic, was made around 1400–1520 by a craftsman in Aztec Mexico.*

How to use this book

Background information on each mosaic featured, including its designer, date, location, and history

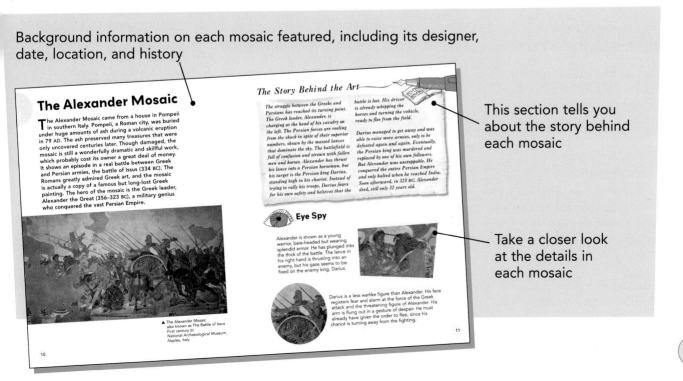

This section tells you about the story behind each mosaic

Take a closer look at the details in each mosaic

How are mosaics made?

The ancient Greeks pioneered a basic form of mosaic. Around 800 BC, they started arranging pebbles of different colors into pictures. Later, they painted some of the pebbles to brighten the **composition**, achieving strikingly bold results. Pebble mosaics are still often used, especially for outdoor settings, such as formal gardens and yards.

▲ *This pebble mosaic from Pella in Greece dates from the fourth century BC. The stones have not been worked on, but keep their natural shapes. Although it is ancient, the design looks like something from a modern garden!*

The Greeks and Romans soon found that, if they wanted more detailed mosaic pictures, they had to use smaller stones that fitted closely together. So mosaic makers cut the stones into little cubes and other shapes needed to follow the outlines in the picture. These small pieces were known by the Latin name *tesserae*. A cement and sand mixture, called **grout**, stuck the sides together. Rubbed down and polished, the flat surfaces of the tesserae created a pleasing and practical floor decoration.

Mosaics were too heavy to use on walls and ceilings until the first century BC when a lightweight glass was introduced and replaced stones for many purposes. The glass was colored, or was made to look golden by putting gold foil inside it. Set at angles to catch the light, the gilded backgrounds of church mosaics created dazzling effects.

Working methods

Mosaic artists have used two main working methods. The **direct method** is to draw the design on the plaster or other **adhesive** backing. Then the bases of the stones are set directly into place. The **indirect**, or **reverse method**, is slower, but gives the artist greater control. It involves using a full-scale guide drawing called a **cartoon**. The drawing is done as a reverse or mirror image of the final work. Following the design, the tesserae are lightly pasted, face down, onto the cartoon. It is then cut into sections. Each section is turned upside down onto a board. Then the assembled tesserae are slid into their permanent cement base. When cartoon and paste are washed off, the image is seen the right way around.

▲ This wall mosaic was designed by Shug Jones and Lynne Chinn in 2005. Called Tracks of Our Past and Future, it is 75.5 ft. (23 m) long and celebrates the African-American Douglass Community of Plano, Texas

Modern mosaic artists try to achieve all kinds of effects. They may work with unusual materials, such as shells, pottery, or mother-of-pearl, or they may use manufactured glass and other commercial products.

The tools used to create mosaics, though now made by machines, have hardly changed over the centuries. Only a few jobs, such as rubbing down and polishing, are no longer done by hand. The talent and skill of the mosaic artist remain as important as ever.

The Alexander Mosaic

The Alexander Mosaic came from a house in Pompeii in southern Italy. Pompeii, a Roman city, was buried under huge amounts of ash during a volcanic eruption in 79 AD. The ash preserved many treasures that were only uncovered centuries later. Though damaged, the mosaic is still a wonderfully dramatic and skillful work, which probably cost its owner a great deal of money. It shows an episode in a real battle between Greek and Persian armies, the battle of Issus (334 BC). The Romans greatly admired Greek art, and the mosaic is actually a copy of a famous but long-lost Greek painting. The hero of the mosaic is the Greek leader, Alexander the Great (356–323 BC), a military genius who conquered the vast Persian Empire.

▲ The Alexander Mosaic
also known as The Battle of Issus
First century BC
National Archaeological Museum,
Naples, Italy

The Story Behind the Art

The struggle between the Greeks and Persians has reached its turning point. The Greek leader, Alexander, is charging at the head of his cavalry on the left. The Persian forces are reeling from the shock in spite of their superior numbers, shown by the massed lances that dominate the sky. The battlefield is full of confusion and strewn with fallen men and horses. Alexander has thrust his lance into a Persian horseman, but his target is the Persian king Darius, standing high in his chariot. Instead of trying to rally his troops, Darius fears for his own safety and believes that the battle is lost. His driver is already whipping the horses and turning the vehicle, ready to flee from the field.

Darius managed to get away and was able to raise more armies, only to be defeated again and again. Eventually, the Persian king was murdered and replaced by one of his own followers. But Alexander was unstoppable. He conquered the entire Persian Empire and only halted when he reached India. Soon afterward, in 323 BC, Alexander died, still only 32 years old.

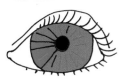 ## Eye Spy

Alexander is shown as a young warrior, bare-headed but wearing splendid armor. He has plunged into the thick of the battle. The lance in his right hand is thrusting into an enemy, but his gaze seems to be fixed on the enemy king, Darius.

Darius is a less warlike figure than Alexander. His face registers fear and alarm at the force of the Greek attack and the threatening figure of Alexander. His arm is flung out in a gesture of despair. He must already have given the order to flee, since his chariot is turning away from the fighting.

North by Northwest

This brilliantly colored mosaic shows a scene from the famous movie *North by Northwest*, made in 1959. It belongs to a set of 17 mosaics in Leytonstone **tube station**, an underground railroad station in London, England. Eighty thousand glass tiles were used on the mosaics, which took seven months to complete. They celebrate the life and work of the movie director Alfred Hitchcock (1899–1980), who was born in the area. Hitchcock was often described as "the master of suspense," because his movies are full of surprises and keep viewers wondering what will happen next. *North by Northwest* is regarded as one of his best works, mixing comedy with thrills. The episode of the crop-spraying plane, shown here, is one of its most dramatic moments.

▲ North by Northwest
Greenwich Mural Workshop
2001
Leytonstone Underground Station, London, England

The Story Behind the Art

The scene is a cornfield in Illinois. Roger Thornhill is running for his life as a plane swoops to attack him. Roger has been in deep trouble for some time. A harmless businessman, he has been mistaken for a U.S. government agent and framed for murder. Now he is being pursued by both the police and a ruthless gang of spies.

At the beginning of this episode, Roger arrives at an empty crossroads. He expects to meet the government agent he has been mistaken for, and hopes to clear things up. In the far distance, a biplane is crop-dusting (spraying pesticides to prevent insects destroying the crops). To do its job, a crop-duster must fly low over the fields. So neither Roger nor the audience takes any notice of the plane as it steadily approaches, until a machine gun starts firing. Roger realizes he has been led into a trap. He is out in the open with nowhere to hide. He runs through the fields, desperately dodging bullets and hoping for a way out...

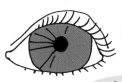 Eye Spy

Red and black tesserae create a vivid, radiating impact, making it look as though the plane's propellers are whirring around.

The ground behind Roger is colorfully patterned. But its increasingly small tesserae and long, inward-slanting lines are also important in giving a sense of distance and movement to Roger's forward rush.

From close up, Thornhill's face is made up of extraordinary colors. But from a distance, they blend very effectively, capturing both his fear and his determination.

The Judgement of Paris

*T*he *Judgement of Paris* was originally part of a large and beautiful mosaic floor in Antioch, a city in Syria that belonged to the Roman Empire. The story is one of the many Greek myths and legends that the Romans also enjoyed. Most of the characters in these stories can be called by their Greek or their Roman names. For example, the Greek goddesses Athene, Hera, and Aphrodite are also known by the Roman names Athena, Minerva, and Venus. The story behind *The Judgement of Paris* belongs to a large group of linked tales about how the legendary Trojan War broke out and what happened during and after it.

◀ The Judgement of Paris *Second century* AD *Louvre Museum, Paris, France*

The Story Behind the Art

The young shepherd Paris is faced with a difficult decision. He must judge which of three goddesses is the most beautiful. In the picture, Paris is seated, thinking. Beside him is the messenger of the gods, Hermes, who has given Paris his task. The goddesses are placed in front of the young man and are trying to influence his choice. Warlike Athene (far left) offers him military glory if he chooses her. In the center, Hera, wife of the king of the gods, sits on a throne. She tells Paris that if he chooses her, he will rule Asia. Aphrodite, goddess of love, stands at the right, in a lovely blue gown. Her offer is the love of the most beautiful woman in the world. Faced with a choice between fame, power, and love, Paris decides that love is what he wants. He chooses Aphrodite.

Afterward, all goes well for Paris for a time. He is recognized as a long-lost son of the king of Troy. He becomes a prince and is sent on a mission to the Greek city of Sparta. There he meets Sparta's beautiful queen, Helen, who is married to King Menelaus. As Aphrodite promised, Helen falls in love with Paris and runs away with him to Troy.

Then the romance turns into tragedy. The Greeks, feeling insulted, assemble an army to recover Helen and take revenge on Paris. They sail for Troy and besiege it for ten years. Many men die during the war, and at its end, the city of Troy is a smoking ruin.

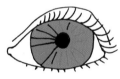 **Eye Spy**

A little goat drinks from a pool. The blue glass of the pool creates the shimmering look of water.

The winged sandals identify Hermes (Roman name Mercury) as the swift messenger of the gods. He also carries a special staff, the **caduceus**, with a serpent wrapped around it.

Eros (Roman name Cupid) is the child of Aphrodite. His presence signals her victory in the contest.

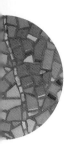

Noah's Ark

The spread of the Christian religion from the first century AD meant that many new stories were told through art. By the fourth century, mosaics in many parts of Europe and the Near East were showing scenes from the **Old Testament** and the lives of Jesus and the Apostles and saints. During the **Middle Ages**, the city of Venice, in the northeast of Italy, became especially wealthy and powerful through trade. Its great church of St. Mark's is filled with wonderful mosaics telling famous religious stories. The one shown here belongs to a series of episodes about the life of Noah. Mosaics, such as these, are not as realistic as the Roman examples we have seen. The artist emphasizes their spiritual meaning, for example, by setting the action against a gold background, which creates an otherworldly atmosphere.

◄ Noah Taking the Birds into the Ark
Thirteenth century
St. Mark's Church, Venice, Italy

The Story Behind the Art

Long ago, God was angered by the evil way that people lived. He decided to send a flood that would destroy all life on earth. But there was one righteous man named Noah, so God decided to spare him. He told Noah how to build an ark that would protect him and his family when the flood began. Noah was instructed to take into the ark a male and a female of every living creature. This meant that no species would perish. Artists particularly liked this part of the story, which allowed them to portray every kind of animal they could think of!

Here, Noah and his family are ready to go on board. Noah himself is putting a pair of eagles inside, while (left to right) ravens, storks, pelicans, herons, and hooded crows wait for their turn.

When the rains and gushing springs poured down on earth, the ark floated on the rising waters. Later, when the flood began to go down, the ark came to rest on the top of a mountain. Noah released a dove. At first, it found no land to settle on and came back to the ark. But at the third try, the dove flew off and never returned. It had made a home for itself, and that meant the waters had rolled back and it was safe to leave the ark. So Noah, his family, and all the creatures went out and started life on earth again.

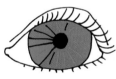 **Eye Spy**

Noah has picked up a pair of sea eagles and is putting them into the ark. The artist has accurately observed all of the birds in the mosaic.

The hooded crows at the end of the line stand out brilliantly against the gold background, which gives many medieval pictures their otherworldly atmosphere.

Noah's sons and their wives will sail in the ark—though here they don't look completely happy about the idea!

Defiance

The National Gallery in London has Britain's largest national collection of paintings. But the first works of art on show are marble mosaics at the main entrance. Many people don't notice them, because the entrance is usually crowded and the mosaics are on the floor under their feet! The mosaics celebrate Britain and the British way of life. They are all by the Russian-born artist, Boris Anrep (1883–1969), a mosaic specialist who designed and made the works in his Paris **studio**. *Defiance* belongs to a group of mosaics that Anrep called "The Modern Virtues." It was directly inspired by Britain's part in World War II.

◀ Defiance
Boris Anrep
1952
National Gallery,
London, England

The Story Behind the Art

Defiance records a historic moment in the early part of World War II (1939–45). In 1940, Germany defeated France and Britain. France was forced to surrender, and Britain was left to face a mighty enemy who ruled most of Europe. Britain's prime minister, Winston Churchill, declared that Britain would keep fighting, and he expressed the nation's determination in a series of great speeches.

Anrep's mosaic shows Churchill standing in front of the white cliffs of Dover, symbolizing Britain. He wears his most famous wartime outfit—a helmet and overalls (very unusual at a time when upper-class people usually wore suits

in public). He raises his left hand, making a "V for Victory" sign; his right hand is clenched in a fist. The other figure, dominating a conquered Europe, stands for Nazi Germany and its leader, Adolf Hitler. It is shown as a monster, dancing with rage at Churchill's refusal to submit.

During this period, British fighter planes defeated the Germans in the air during the **Battle of Britain**. *Britain also withstood heavy bombing (* **the Blitz** *). Then in 1941, Russia and the United States were drawn into the war on Britain's side. The strength of the two sides changed dramatically, dooming Germany and its allies.*

Eye Spy

The monster is in the shape of the swastika symbol used by the Nazis on flags, uniforms, and **insignia**. The creature's frenzy also suggests the famous rages of the Nazi leader, Adolf Hitler.

Coming to power when defeat seemed likely, Churchill often made this encouraging V-for-Victory sign.

The monster stands for Nazi Germany. It is also like the Beast described in biblical prophecies, crowned, with a lion's mouth and bear paws, snarling and shouting.

Odysseus and the Sirens

The most famous ancient Greek poet was a man named Homer, who was believed to have lived in the eighth century BC. According to legend, he was blind, but nothing is really known for certain about him. Homer composed two poems of war and adventure, the *Iliad* and the *Odyssey*. The *Iliad* is about heroic battles and duels during the Trojan War. The *Odyssey* is a kind of sequel. It follows the adventures of one of the Greek leaders, Odysseus, as he tries to make his way home after the war. Odysseus was clever and cunning, as the story of the Sirens shows. But he was forced to wander for years before he was able to return to his island kingdom. The Romans liked and pictured episodes from the story of Odysseus, whom they called Ulysses. The mosaic below comes from Tunisia in what was once Roman North Africa.

▲ Odysseus and the Sirens
Third century AD
Bardo Museum, Tunis, Tunisia

The Story Behind the Art

Odysseus stands tied to the mast of his ship, which is passing the island where the Sirens live. These strange creatures have beautiful human faces, wings, and birdlike legs and clawed feet. They are monsters who sing an enchanting song that lures passing seafarers to their deaths. One has two flutes, and another holds a lyre.

Then what is the crafty Odysseus doing here? He has been warned about the Sirens, but he wants to hear their fatal song without coming to any harm. So he has told his men to tie him to the mast. They must not release him, however hard he begs, until the ship has passed

on. His men are safe, since their ears are plugged with wax and they cannot hear the song—another of Odysseus' ideas.

But Odysseus does hear the Sirens' song. It promises that he will share the Sirens' knowledge of the past and future if he will come to them. As he feared, Odysseus cannot resist and signals his men to release him. But they follow his instructions, tying him up even more securely until the danger is over and he comes to his senses. Thanks to his cleverness, Odysseus has heard the song of the Sirens and lived to tell the tale.

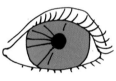 **Eye Spy**

The oars and the waves of the sea are arranged as patterns. They form a strong contrast with the dramatic treatment of the seafarers and the Sirens.

The Siren looks like a human being, but her wings and evil-looking talons give her away.

The hero Odysseus stands upright, tied to the mast. His figure is strongly contrasted with the clumsy, sinister poses of the Sirens.

Make a mosaic pen holder

What you do:

1 Starting at the base of the styrofoam cup, glue on the macaroni shapes one at a time. Build up the pattern in threes to make square tiles. Place the tiles in different directions.

You will need:

styrofoam cup
• *glue* • *glue brush*
• *macaroni shapes*
(dry) • *paints and*
paintbrush

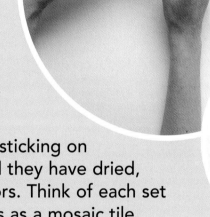

2 When you have finished sticking on the macaroni shapes and they have dried, paint them in bright colors. Think of each set of three macaroni shapes as a mosaic tile, and paint them in different colors.

3 Leave your pen holder to dry.

4 When it is dry, put your pens in it and show it off on your desk!

Make a patterned place mat

You will need:
colored construction paper • letter-sized piece of card • graph paper • scissors • colored pens or pencils • ruler • glue stick • laminator and laminating sheets or self-adhesive plastic sheets

What you do:

1 Draw a rough design for your place mat on graph paper. Why not try a **symmetrical** pattern?

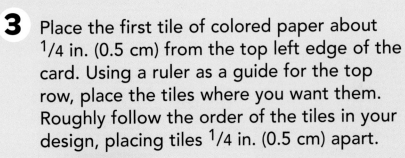

2 Cut the colored construction paper into strips about 1/2 in. (1 cm) wide, and then cut the strips so that you have lots of little tiles. You may want to use a pencil and ruler to mark out the measurements.

3 Place the first tile of colored paper about 1/4 in. (0.5 cm) from the top left edge of the card. Using a ruler as a guide for the top row, place the tiles where you want them. Roughly follow the order of the tiles in your design, placing tiles 1/4 in. (0.5 cm) apart.

4 Stick the tiles down on the card with a glue stick as you go.

5 When you're finished making your pattern, you may want to protect it by **laminating** it or covering it with a self-adhesive plastic sheet.

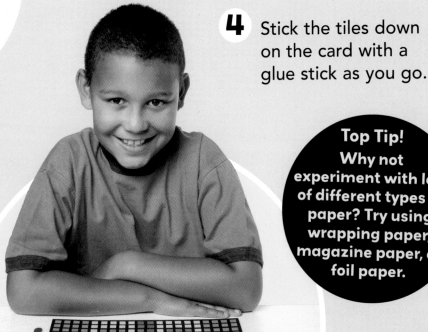

Top Tip!
Why not experiment with lots of different types of paper? Try using wrapping paper, magazine paper, or foil paper.

23

Make a mosaic photo frame

What you do:

1 Decide what shape you want your frame to be: square, circular, or maybe something more unusual. Sketch it on the cereal box card. Don't forget to include the hole for the photo!

2 Cut out your frame using scissors. You may need an adult to help you to cut the central hole.

Top Tip!
You can try using lots of different materials to decorate your frame. What about glass beads, pebbles, bottle tops, or shells?

3 Arrange the collection of buttons around the frame until you're happy with the result. It doesn't matter if some stick out over the edge—in fact, it adds to the effect! Be careful not to cover the central hole.

4 Stick the buttons on with glue.

5 Turn your frame on its front and apply some glue around the edges of the photo hole. Lay your photo face down over the hole and press it down firmly.

6 Stick some ribbon or string on the back of your frame using strong tape.

7 Hang up your frame.

Make a wall border

What you do:

1 Cut out a piece of wall lining paper using safety scissors. It could be letter or tabloid size, depending on the wall space available.

2 Sketch the design you want to feature on the wall lining paper. Why not do this activity with friends or classmates and create a scene from Noah's Ark, like the one on page 16?

like the one on page 16?

You will need:
wall lining paper • different colored paper
• *safety scissors*
• *glue stick • pencil*
• *self-adhesive plastic*

3 Cut or tear squares of different-colored paper and keep each color in a separate pile.

4 Position and glue the tiles onto your sketch. You may have to cut some of the pieces to fit.

5 Cover your completed picture with self-adhesive plastic to protect it.

6 Put all the different pictures together to create a long wall border.

Glossary

abstract   In art, this describes works (pictures, sculptures, etc.) that consist of colors and shapes, without any recognizable figures or objects.

adhesive   Any substance that sticks one thing to another.

Battle of Britain   War in the air, waged in the summer of 1940 between the attacking Germans and Britain's royal Air Force (RAF).

Blitz (the)   The nickname given to the very heavy bombing of British cities during World War II.

caduceus   The staff carried by the Greek god Hermes (called Mercury by the Romans.)

cartoon   Full-scale drawing, made as part of an artist's preparation for a mosaic, painting, or other work.

composition   The way a picture is arranged to make it pleasing or striking.

direct method   The simplest method of creating a mosaic, by drawing a design on a surface and putting tesserae directly onto it.

grout   An adhesive mixture of sand and cement, inserted between tiles or tesserae.

indirect method   See reverse method.

insignia   Badges or symbols.

laminating   Covering and bonding with a thin, transparent sheet of plastic.

Middle Ages   The period of European history between about 500 and 1500 AD.

myths   Stories about the long-distant past, usually including legends about the creation of the world and human beings. Myths often feature gods, heroes, and monsters.

Old Testament   The oldest part of the Bible. It describes the history and religion of the Jewish people in ancient times.

reverse method   Method of creating a mosaic, using a mirror-image drawing or cartoon.

studio   The place where an artist works.

symmetrical   Describes a design or object that is exactly balanced, so that, for example, both halves are the same shape and color.

tesserae   Small, fairly regular pieces of stone, glass, and ceramic, used to make a mosaic. The singular (just one piece) is tessera.

tube station   A station on London's Underground railroad in England.

Find out more

Books to read

Amazing Mosaics by Sarah Kelly (Barron's Educational, 2000)
Classic Mosaic by Elaine M. Goodwin (Apple Press, 2001)
Design Sourcebook: Mosaics by Martin Cheek (Trafalgar Square Books, 1998)
Mosaic Techniques and Traditions by Sonia King (Sterling, 2006)
Step By Step: Mosaics by Michelle Powell (Heinemann, 2004)
The Complete Pebble Mosaic Handbook by Maggy Howarth (Firefly, 2003)
The Mosaic Artist's Bible by Theresa Mills (Trafalgar Square Books, 2005)

Websites to visit

Due to the changing nature of Internet links, PowerKids Press has developed an online list of Web sites related to the subject of this book. This site is updated regularly. Please use this link to access this list:
www.powerkidslinks.com/sia/mosaic

Places to go

Gallery 66.US, New Mexico, features work from more than 30 mosaic artists from the US, Canada, Australia, and New Zealand.

NYC Subway, New York, features mosaics dating from 1910, as well as modern installations by contemporary mosaic artists.

See the Native American Mosaic Warrior at the Woolaroc Museum, Oklahoma, plus a collection of Aztec Mosaic masks.

The Metropolitan Museum of Art, New York, has a permanent mosaic collection featuring Roman and Islamic mosaics, plus pieces by Louis Comfort Tiffany.

The Mosaic Sculpture Garden, Washington, has a great selection of large mosaic sculptures by contemporary mosaic artist Jack Lewis.

View the impressive mosaic mirror exterior of the American Visionary Art Museum, Maryland.

Index

Photos or pictures are shown below in bold, **like this**.

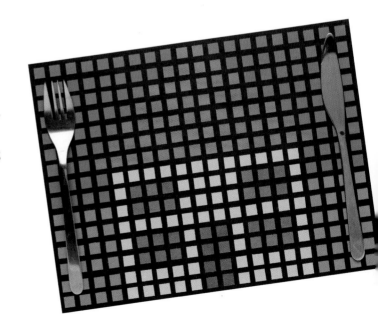